Python3 101 MCQ - Multiple Choice Questions Answers, Tests and Quizzes

By S. C. Lewis

Version: 0.02

Multiple Choice Questions for Python 3

101 MCQ's for Python Jobs, Tests & Quizzes

If you are learning Python programming on your own (whether you are learning from Python books, videos or online tutorials and lesson plans) this book is for you. These questions and answers can be used to test your knowledge of Python3. If you already know Python, you can still use it to check how many questions you can attempt on your own without any help. You may want to go through these questions before you appear for a job interview. If you are a teacher or tutor who is teaching Python, you'll find these MCQ useful as a tool to understand how much your students have learned what you have taught.

All these questions are based on **Python 3** and the target level of questions is Beginner Level - someone who is just starting to learn Python or someone who has recently learnt Python. Answer Key for these questions is provided at the end.

S.C. Lewis

FAQ

Q 1. These questions are based on which version of Python?
Ans: All the MCQ for this book are based on Python 3.

Q 2. The questions have been tested on which platforms?
Ans: These questions have been tested with Python 3.4.0 on Linux and Windows operating systems. You might want to download/update the newest Python version from www.Python.org for your own system before attempting these questions.

Q 3. I have just started to learn Python. Will I be able to answer these questions?
Ans: The questions for this book are written for beginners level and are intended for someone who has recently learnt Python. Someone who has just started to learn Python is likely to find these questions useful too.

Q 4. When I run the statements given in the question, I am not able to get any of the 4 options as my output?
Ans: It is recommended that you try to run the statements for which some output is expected by saving them as a program in the IDLE File Editor only (unless noted otherwise) and if it not works as expected then only try it in IDLE shell (one statement at a time). In some rare cases, it might be because of the version of Python you are using and your operating system as some questions might give platform specific output.

Q 5. When I run the statements given in the question, the output is not in the same order or exactly same as the given answer?
Ans: This is because some statements and functions give a random output or an unsorted order of items. In such cases, you may select the answer which is most likely to be the possible answer based on your understanding of Python.

Q 6. What is the recommended approach to solve these questions?
Ans: The best approach to solve these questions is to take a pen(or pencil) & paper and try attempting these questions one by one.
1. If you do not know the answer to a particular question (may be you have not learnt the topic yet), you may leave the answer for that question blank, skip that question for the moment and come back to attempt it after you have learnt that topic.

2. If you attempted a question but your answer was wrong, go through your Python notes (or books) again and then re-attempt that question later when you have thoroughly grasped that concept.

3. If you get all the answers right in your first attempt, Congratulations! you are doing something right. You can still come back to these questions after a while for revision and to keep those topics and the related concepts in your memory refreshed.

Q 7. Does the answer key contains the explanations to these questions too?

Ans: The answer key contains only the answers and does not contain the explanation to the answers. This is because most of the answers are self-explantory or very simple to understand if you have understood the basic concepts well. If you still face some difficulty, try thinking for a while and you'll know why. Or else, you might Google that statement or expression and you are likely to find your explanation easily but you might not need to go that far. If you still face any problems, feel free to let me know.

Python MCQ

1. What will be the output after the following statements?

   ```
   m = 28
   n = 5
   print(m // n)
   ```

   a. 5.0
   b. 6
   c. 5
   d. 4.0

2. What will be the output after the following statements?

   ```
   m = 90
   n = 7
   print(m % n)
   ```

   a. 6
   b. 4
   c. 6.0
   d. 5.0

3. What will be the output after the following statements?

   ```
   m = 79
   n = 64
   print(m < n)
   ```

   a. m < n
   b. False
   c. True
   d. No

4. What will be the output after the following statements?

   ```
   m = 92
   n = 35
   print(m > n)
   ```

   a. True
   b. False
   c. Yes
   d. No

5. What will be the output after the following statements?

   ```
   m = False
   ```

n = True
print(m and n)

a. m and n
b. False
c. True
d. mn

6.   What will be the output after the following statements?

m = True
n = False
print(m or n)

a. m or n
b. False
c. True
d. mn

7.   What will be the output after the following statements?

m = True
n = False
print(not m)

a. not m
b. False
c. True
d. Not defined

8.   What will be the output after the following statements?

m = True
n = False
print('not n')

a. not n
b. False
c. True
d. Not defined

9.   What will be the output after the following statements?

m = 7 * 5 + 8
print(m)

a. 91
b. 20
c. 47
d. 43

10.   What will be the output after the following statements?

m = 9 * (3 + 12)
print(m)

a. 45
b. 159
c. 95
d. 135

11.   What will be the output after the following statements?

m = '40' + '01'
print(m)

a. 4001
b. 01
c. 41
d. 40

12.   What will be the output after the following statements?

m = 81 + 34
print(m)

a. 8134
b. 81
c. 115
d. 34

13.   What will be the data type of n after the following statements if the user entered the number 45?

m = input('Enter a number: ')
n = int(m)

a. Float
b. String
c. List
d. Integer

14.   What is the data type of m after the following statement?

m = (41, 54, 23, 68)

a. Dictionary
b. Tuple
c. String
d. List

15.   What is the data type of m after the following statement?

m = ['July', 'September', 'December']

a. Dictionary
b. Tuple
c. List
d. String

16.   What will be the output after the following statements?

m = ['July', 'September', 'December']
n = m[1]
print(n)

a. ['July', 'September', 'December']
b. July
c. September
d. December

17.   What will be the output after the following statements?

m = [45, 51, 67]
n = m[2]
print(n)

a. 67
b. 51
c. [45, 51, 67]
d. 45

18.   What will be the output after the following statements?

m = [75, 23, 64]
n = m[0] + m[1]
print(n)

a. 75
b. 23
c. 64
d. 98

19.   What will be the output after the following statements?

m = ['July', 'September', 'December']
n = m[0] + m[2]
print(n)

a. July

b. JulyDecember
c. JulySeptember
d. SeptemberDecember

20.   What will be the output after the following statements?

m = 17
n = 5
o = m * n
print(o)

a. m * n
b. 17
c. 85
d. 5

21.   What will be the output after the following statements?

m = [25, 34, 70, 63]
n = m[2] - m[0]
print(n)

a. 25
b. 45
c. 70
d. 34

22.   What will be the output after the following statements?

m = [25, 34, 70, 63]
n = str(m[1]) +str(m[2])
print(n)

a. 2534
b. 95
c. 104
d. 3470

23.   What will be the data type of m after the following statement?

m = [90, 'A', 115, 'B', 250]

a. List
b. String
c. Dictionary
d. Tuple

24.   What will be the data type of m after the following statement?

m = 'World Wide Web'

a. List
b. String
c. Dictionary
d. Tuple

25.   What will be the data type of m after the following statement?

m = {'Listen' :'Music', 'Play' : 'Games'}

a. List
b. Set
c. Dictionary
d. Tuple

26.   What will be the data type of m after the following statement?

m = {'A', 'F', 'R', 'Y'}

a. List
b. Set
c. Dictionary
d. Tuple

27.   What will be the data type of m after the following statement?

m = True

a. List
b. String
c. Dictionary
d. Boolean

28.   What will be the data type of m after the following statements?

true = "Honesty is the best policy"
m = true

a. List
b. String
c. Dictionary
d. Boolean

29.   What will be the output after the following statements?

m = {'Listen' :'Music', 'Play' : 'Games'}
print(m.keys())

a. dict_keys(['Play', 'Listen'])
b. dict_keys(['Music', 'Games'])

c. dict_keys({'Listen' :'Music', 'Play' : 'Games'})
d. dict_keys({'Listen' : 'Games'})

30.   What will be the output after the following statements?

m = {'Listen' :'Music', 'Play' : 'Games'}
print(m.values())

a. dict_values(['Play', 'Listen'])
b. dict_values(['Games', 'Music'])
c. dict_values({'Listen' :'Music', 'Play' : 'Games'})
d. dict_values({'Listen' : 'Games'})

31.   What will be the output after the following statements?

m = {'Listen' :'Music', 'Play' : 'Games'}
n = m['Play']
print(n)

a. Listen
b. Music
c. Play
d. Games

32.   What will be the output after the following statements?

m = {'Listen' :'Music', 'Play' : 'Games'}
n = list(m.values())
print(n[0])

a. Listen
b. Music
c. Play
d. Games

33.   What will be the output after the following statements?

m = {'Listen' :'Music', 'Play' : 'Games'}
n = list(m.items())
print(n)

a. [('Play', 'Games'), ('Listen', 'Music')]
b. [('Listen', 'Music')]
c. [('Play', 'Games')]
d. ('Play', 'Games'), ('Listen', 'Music')

34.   What will be the output after the following statements?

m = 36
if m > 19:

print(100)

a. 36
b. 19
c. 100
d. m

35.   What will be the output after the following statements?

m = 50
if m > 50:
        print(25)
else:
        print(75)

a. 50
b. m
c. 75
d. 25

36.   What will be the output after the following statements?

m = 8
if m > 7:
        print(50)
elif m == 7:
        print(60)
else:
        print(70)

a. 50
b. 60
c. 70
d. 8

37.   What will be the output after the following statements?

m = 85
n = 17
print(m / n)

a. 5
b. 5.5
c. 6.0
d. 5.0

38.   What will be the output after the following statements?

m = 44
n = 23

```
m = m + n
print(m)
```

a. 23
b. 44
c. 67
d. m + n

39.   What will be the output after the following statements?

```
m = 20
n = 6
m = m * n
print(m)
```

a. m * n
b. 20
c. 206
d. 120

40.   What will be the output after the following statements?

```
m = 99
n = 11
m = m - n
print(m)
```

a. 88
b. 11
c. 99
d. 9911

41.   What will be the output after the following statements?

```
m = 70
n = 10
m = m % n
print(m)
```

a. 7
b. 70
c. 10
d. 0

42.   What will be the output after the following statements?

```
m = 57
n = 19
o = m == n
print(o)
```

a. 19
b. True
c. False
d. 57

43.   What will be the output after the following statements?

```
m = 33
if m > 33:
      print('A')
elif m == 30:
      print('B')
else:
      print('C')
```

a. C
b. B
c. A
d. 33

44.   What will be the output after the following statements?

```
m = 99
if m > 9  and m < 19:
      print('AA')
elif m > 19  and m < 39:
      print('BB')
elif m > 39  and m < 59:
      print('CC')
else:
      print('DD')
```

a. CC
b. DD
c. BB
d. AA

45.   What will be the output after the following statements?

```
m = 200
if m <= 25 or m >= 200:
      print('AA')
elif m <= 45 or m >= 150:
      print('BB')
elif m <= 65 or m >= 100:
      print('CC')
else:
      print('DD')
```

a. CC
b. DD
c. BB
d. AA

46.   What will be the output after the following statements?

```
m = 6
while m < 11:
     print(m, end='')
     m = m + 1
```

a. 6789
b. 5678910
c. 678910
d. 56789

47.   What will be the output after the following statements?

```
m = 2
while m < 5:
     print(m, end='')
     m += 2
```

a. 24
b. 246
c. 2468
d. 248

48.   What will be the output after the following statements?

```
m = 1
n = 5
while n + m < 8:
     m += 1
     print(m, end='')
```

a. 123
b. 23
c. 234
d. 2345

49.   What will be the output after the following statements?

```
m, n = 2, 5
while n < 10:
     print(n, end='')
     m, n = n, m + n
```

a. 25

b. 58
c. 579
d. 57

50.   What will be the output after the following statements?

m = 'ABC'
for i in m:
       print(i, end=' ')

a. A
b. ABC
c. A B C
d. I

51.   What will be the output after the following statements?

for m in range(7):
       print(m, end='')

a. 0123456
b. 01234567
c. 123456
d. 1234567

52.   What will be the output after the following statements?

for m in range(6,9):
       print(m, end='')

a. 67
b. 678
c. 6789
d. 5678

53.   What will be the output after the following statements?

for m in range(2,9,3):
       print(m, end='')

a. 293
b. 369
c. 239
d. 258

54.   What will be the output after the following statements?

m = ('m', 'n', 'o', 'p')
for n in m:
       print(n, end=' ')

a. n
b. mnop
c. m n o p
d. ('m', 'n', 'o', 'p')

55.   What will be the output after the following statements?

```
m = {'m', 'n', 'o', 'p'}
if 'n' in m:
        print('n', end=' ')
```

a. n
b. mnop
c. m n o p
d. {'m', 'n', 'o', 'p'}

56.   What will be the output after the following statements?

```
m = {45 : 75, 55 : 85}
for i in m:
        print(i, end=' ')
```

a. 45 : 75
b. 45 55
c. 55 : 85
d. 75 85

57.   What will be the output after the following statements?

```
m = {45 : 75, 55 : 85}
for n, o in m.items():
        print(n, o, end=' ')
```

a. 45 : 75, 55 : 85
b. {45 : 75, 55 : 85}
c. 45 55 75 85
d. 45 75 55 85

58.   What will be the output after the following statements?

```
for m in range(6,9):
        print(m, end='')
      if m == 8:
            break
```

a. 67
b. 679
c. 678
d. 6789

59.   What will be the output after the following statements?

```
for m in range(6,9):
    if m == 8:
        continue
    print(m, end='')
```

a. 67
b. 679
c. 678
d. 6789

60.   What will be the output after the following statements?

```
m = [15, 65, 105]
n = 5 in m
print(n)
```

a. 15
b. [15, 65, 105]
c. True
d. False

61.   What will be the output after the following statements?

```
m = 18
def nop() :
     print(m)
nop()
```

a. m
b. nop
c. 18
d. mnop

62.   What will be the output after the following statements?

```
def abc(m, n) :
     print(m - n)
abc(14, 5)
```

a. (14, 5)
b. 145
c. m - n
d. 9

63.   What will be the output after the following statements?

```
def abc(m=15, n=10, o=5) :
```

```
        print(m * n + o)
    abc()
```

a. 150
b. 155
c. 0
d. 225

64.   What will be the output after the following statements?

```
def abc(m, n) :
    return m * n
print(abc(7, 3))
```

a. 21
b. 7, 3
c. (7, 3)
d. m * n

65.   What will be the output after the following statements?

```
def p(m, n) :
    return m / n
o = p(50, 5)
print(o)
```

a. 5
b. 50 / 5
c. 10.0
d. 10

66.   What will be the output after the following statements?

```
m = {'Listen' :'Music', 'Play' : 'Games'}
n = m['Music']
print(n)
```

a. Music
b. KeyError
c. m['Music']
d. Listen

67.   What will be the output after the following statements?

```
m = lambda n: n**3
print(m(6))
```

a. 6
b. 18
c. 36

d. 216

68.   What does the following statement do?

import os

a. Displays the operating system name and version
b. Imports the os module
c. Imports the os function
d. Imports the directory named os

69.   What will be the output after the following statements?

m = 'Play'
n = 'Games'
print(n + m)

a. Play
b. Games
c. PlayGames
d. GamesPlay

70.   What will be the output after the following statements?

m = 'Play'
n = m * 2
print(n)

a. PlayPlay
b. Play
c. Play2
d. Play*2

71.   What will be the output after the following statements?

m = 'Play Games'
n = m[6]
print(n)

a. m[6]
b. Play Games
c. a
d. G

72.   What will be the output after the following statements?

m = 'Play Games'
n = m[7:9]
print(n)

a. ame
b. Play Games
c. Game
d. me

73.   What will be the output after the following statements?

m = 'Play Games'
n = m[:]
print(n)

a. ame
b. Play Games
c. Play
d. Games

74.   What does the following statement do?

m = open('games.txt', 'r')

a. Opens an existing text file named games.txt to read
b. Opens an existing text file named games.txt to write
c. Opens a new file named games.txt to read
d. Opens an existing text file named games.txt to append

75.   What does the following statement do?

m = open('games.txt', 'w')

a. Opens a new file named games.txt to write
b. Opens or creates a text file named games.txt to write
c. Opens or creates a text file named games.txt to read
d. Opens or creates a text file named games.txt to append

76.   What does the following statement do?

x = open('games.txt', 'a')

a. Opens a new file named games.txt to append
b. Opens or creates a text file named games.txt to write
c. Opens or creates a text file named games.txt to read
d. Opens or creates a text file named games.txt to append

77.   Who is the creator of Python?

a. Albert Einstein
b. Monty Python
c. Leonardo da Vinci
d. Guido Van Rossum

78.   What will be the output after the following statements?

m = False
n = True
o = False
print(m and n and o)

a. m and n
b. True
c. False
d. Error

79.   In the order of precedence, which of the operation will be completed first in the following statement?

7 * 4 + 9 - 2 / 3

a. Addition
b. Subtraction
c. Multiplication
d. Division

80.   In the order of precedence, which of the operation will be completed last in the following statement?

7 * 4 + 9 - 2 / 3

a. Addition
b. Subtraction
c. Multiplication
d. Division

81.   What will be the output after the following statements?

m = 36 / 4 % 2 * 5**3
print(m)

a. 125.0
b. 0
c. 36
d. 14.0

82.   What will be the output after the following statements?

m = 8 / 4 * 10 + 6 **2
print(m)

a. 32
b. 45.0
c. 56.0

d. 0.0

83.   What will be the output after the following statements?

m = [4, 8]
print(m * 3)

a. [4, 8]
b. [4, 8, 4, 8]
c. [4, 8] * 3
d. [4, 8, 4, 8, 4, 8]

84.   What will be the output after the following statements?

m = 67
n = m
m = 72
print(m, n)

a. 67 72
b. 72 67
c. 7267
d. 72 72

85.   What will be the output after the following statements?

m = 20 * 10 // 30
n = 20 * 10.0 // 40
o = 20.0 * 10 / 50
print(m, n, o)

a. 6.5 5.0 4.5
b. 6.0 5.0 4
c. 5 6.0 4.0
d. 6 5.0 4.0

86.   What will be the output after the following statements?

m = 2
for n in range(3, 15, 5):
        n += m + 2
print(n)

a. 14
b. 16
c. 17
d. 19

87.   What will be the output after the following statements?

```
m = False
print(m or not m)
```

a. a
b. False
c. not a
d. True

88.   What will be the output after the following statements?

```
m = min(50, 25, 65, 0, 99)
print(m)
```

a. 0
b. 99
c. 25
d. (50, 25, 65, 0, 99)

89.   What will be the output after the following statements?

```
m = [50, 25, 65, 0, 99]
n = max(m)
print(n)
```

a. 0
b. 99
c. 25
d. (50, 25, 65, 0, 99)

90.   How many times will "Music" be printed after the following statements?

```
for i in range(3, 7):
    print('Music')
```

a. 3
b. 4
c. 5
d. 6

91.   What will be the output after the following statements?

```
m = 39
n = 61
o = (m + n) // 2
print(o)
```

a. 40.0
b. 50.0
c. 50
d. 55

92.   What will be the output after the following statements?

```
m = 10*10**1
print(m)
```

a. 10
b. 1
c. 1000
d. 100

93.   What will be the output after the following statements?

```
m = []
for n in range(6):
        m.append(n*3)
print(m)
```

a. [3, 6, 9, 12, 15]
b. [0, 3, 6, 9, 12]
c. [0, 3, 6, 9, 12, 15]
d. []

94.   What will be the output after the following statements?

```
m = [n*4 for n in range(3)]
print(m)
```

a. [0, 0, 0]
b. [0, 4, 8]
c. [0, 4, 8, 12]
d. [0, 4, 8, 12, 16]

95.   What will be the output after the following statements?

```
m = [-5, -2, 0, 3, 4]
print([n*2 for n in m])
```

a. [-10, -4, 0, 6, 8]
b. [10, 4, 0, 6, 8]
c. [-10, -4, 0, 6]
d. [-10, -4, 0]

96.   What will be the output after the following statements?

```
m = [5, 10, 35]
del m[:]
print(m)
```

a. [5, 10, 35]

b. []
c. [5, 35]
d. 5, 10, 35

97. What will be the output after the following statements?

```
m = 'A'
n = 'B'
o = 'C'
p = [m, n, o]
print(p)
```

a. ['C', 'B', 'A']
b. 'C', 'A', 'B'
c. ['C', 'A', 'B']
d. ['A', 'B', 'C']

98. What will be the output after the following statements?

```
m = list(range(7,10))
print(m)
```

a. [7, 8, 9, 10]
b. list([7, 8, 9])
c. [7, 8, 9]
d. 789

99. What will be the output after the following statements?

```
m = [10, 25, 35]
n = sum(m)
print(n)
```

a. 35
b. 25
c. 10
d. 70

100. What will be the output after the following statements?

```
m = ['Games', 'in', 'Python']
n = 'Play' + m[0] + m[1] + m[2]
print(n)
```

a. PlayGamesinPython
b. Play Games in Python
c. Games in Python
d. GamesinPython

101. What will be the output after the following statements?

```
m = ['Play']
n = ['Games', 'in', 'Python']
o = m + n
print(o)
```

a. ['Games', 'in', 'Python', 'Play']
b. ['Play Games', 'in', 'Python']
c. ['Play', 'Games', 'in', 'Python']
d. ['PlayGames', 'in', 'Python']

<u>Answer Key</u>

1. c
2. a
3. b
4. a
5. b
6. c
7. b
8. a
9. d
10. d
11. a
12. c
13. d
14. b
15. c
16. c
17. a
18. d
19. b
20. c
21. b
22. d
23. a
24. b
25. c
26. b
27. d
28. b
29. a
30. b
31. d
32. b
33. a
34. c
35. c
36. a
37. d
38. c

39. d
40. a
41. d
42. c
43. a
44. b
45. d
46. c
47. a
48. b
49. d
50. c
51. a
52. b
53. d
54. c
55. a
56. b
57. d
58. c
59. a
60. d
61. c
62. d
63. b
64. a
65. c
66. b
67. d
68. b
69. d
70. a
71. c
72. d
73. b
74. a
75. b
76. d
77. d
78. c
79. c
80. b

81. a
82. c
83. d
84. b
85. d
86. c
87. d
88. a
89. b
90. b
91. c
92. d
93. c
94. b
95. a
96. b
97. d
98. c
99. d
100. a
101. c

Thank You

Thanks for buying this book. If you find an errors or have any suggestions, feel free to let me know at sclewis2016@outlook.com

More Books by the Author

If you liked this book, you might want to check the other books by the author too.

Python 3 MCQ - Multiple Choice Questions n Answers for Tests, Quizzes - Python Students & Teachers

Python3 101 MCQ - Multiple Choice Questions Answers for Jobs, Tests and Quizzes

73447429R00020